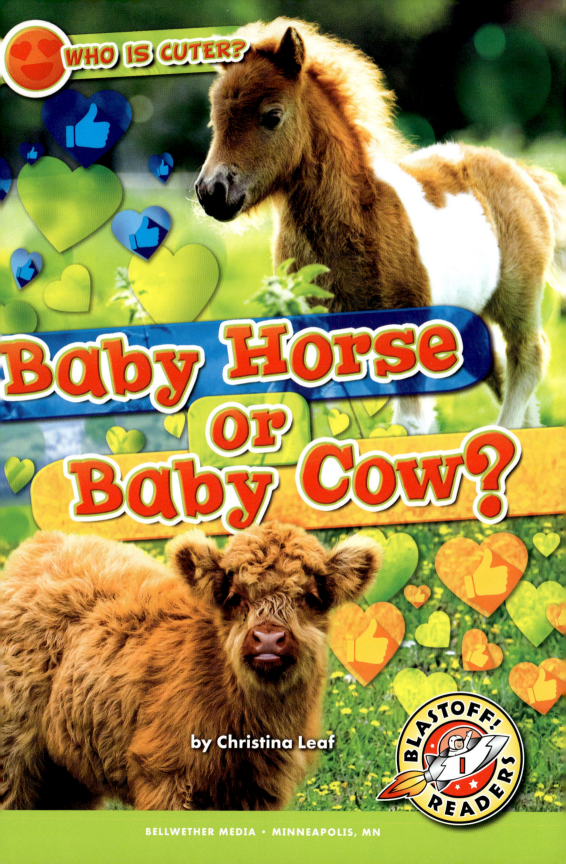

Blastoff! Readers are carefully developed by literacy experts to build reading stamina and move students toward fluency by combining standards-based content with developmentally appropriate text.

 Level 1 provides the most support through repetition of high-frequency words, light text, predictable sentence patterns, and strong visual support.

 Level 2 offers early readers a bit more challenge through varied sentences, increased text load, and text-supportive special features.

 Level 3 advances early-fluent readers toward fluency through increased text load, less reliance on photos, advancing concepts, longer sentences, and more complex special features.

★ **Blastoff! Universe**

This edition first published in 2025 by Bellwether Media, Inc.

No part of this publication may be reproduced in whole or in part without written permission of the publisher. For information regarding permission, write to Bellwether Media, Inc., Attention: Permissions Department, 6012 Blue Circle Drive, Minnetonka, MN 55343.

Library of Congress Cataloging-in-Publication Data

Names: Leaf, Christina, author.
Title: Baby horse or baby cow? / by Christina Leaf.
Description: Minneapolis : Bellwether Media, 2025. | Series: Blastoff! Readers. Who is cuter? | Includes bibliographical references and index. | Audience: Ages 5-8 | Audience: Grades K-1 | Summary: "Developed by literacy experts for students in kindergarten through grade three, this book introduces the differences between baby horses and baby cows to young readers through leveled text and related photos"– Provided by publisher.
Identifiers: LCCN 2024003093 (print) | LCCN 2024003094 (ebook) | ISBN 9798886870312 (library binding) | ISBN 9798893041453 (paperback) | ISBN 9781644878750 (ebook)
Subjects: LCSH: Calves–Juvenile literature. | Foals–Juvenile literature. | Animals–Infancy–Identification–Juvenile literature.
Classification: LCC SF197.5 .L43 2025 (print) | LCC SF197.5 (ebook) | DDC 636/.07–dc23/eng/20240126
LC record available at https://lccn.loc.gov/2024003093
LC ebook record available at https://lccn.loc.gov/2024003094

Text copyright © 2025 by Bellwether Media, Inc. BLASTOFF! READERS and associated logos are trademarks and/or registered trademarks of Bellwether Media, Inc. Bellwether Media is a division of Chrysalis Education Group.

Editor: Suzane Nguyen   Designer: Andrea Schneider

Printed in the United States of America, North Mankato, MN.

Table of Contents

Foals and Calves!	4
Ears and Hooves	8
Stables and Barns	16
Who Is Cuter?	20
Glossary	22
To Learn More	23
Index	24

Foals and Calves!

Baby horses and cows live on farms. Both babies are super cute!

baby cow

baby horse

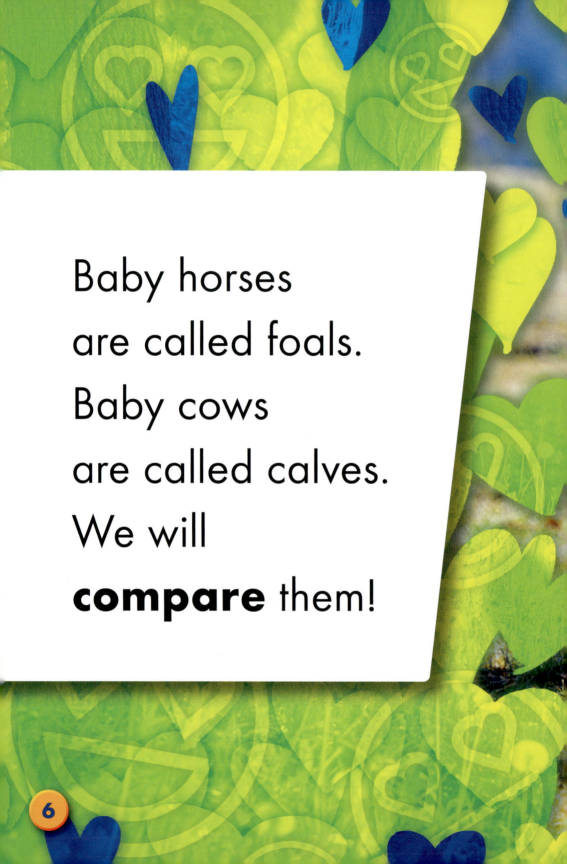

Baby horses are called foals. Baby cows are called calves. We will **compare** them!

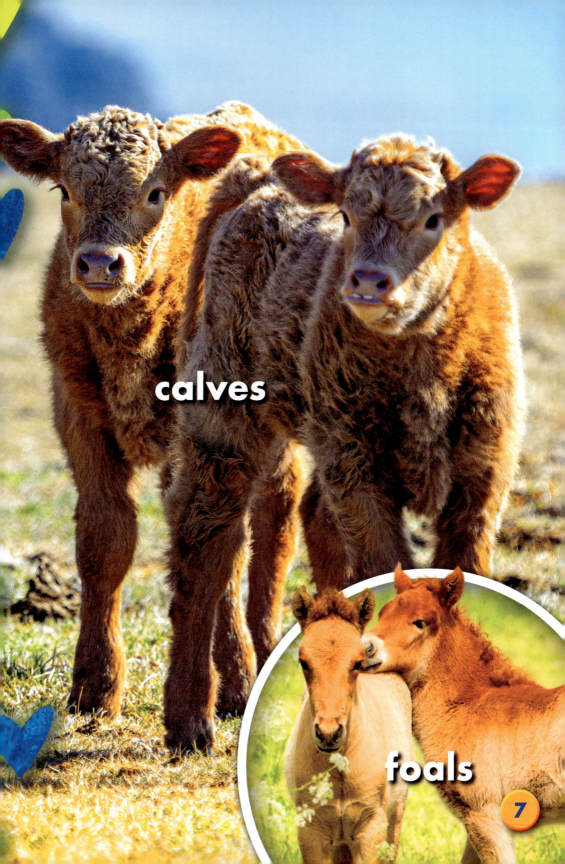
calves

foals

Ears and Hooves

Foals have long, thin faces. Calf faces are shorter and wider.

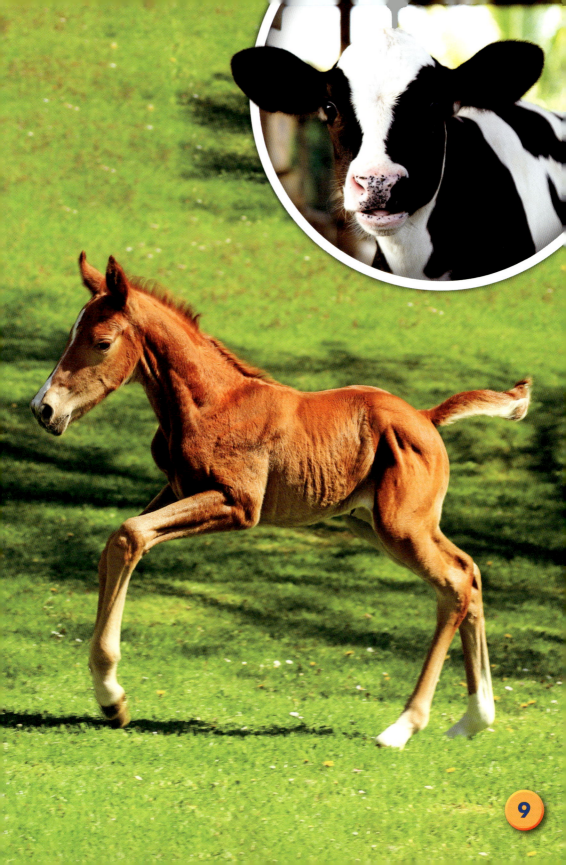

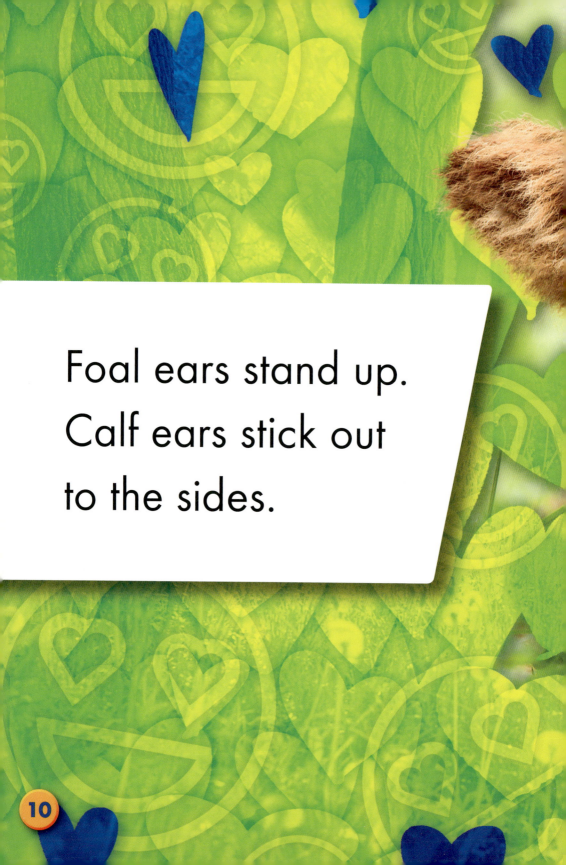

Foal ears stand up. Calf ears stick out to the sides.

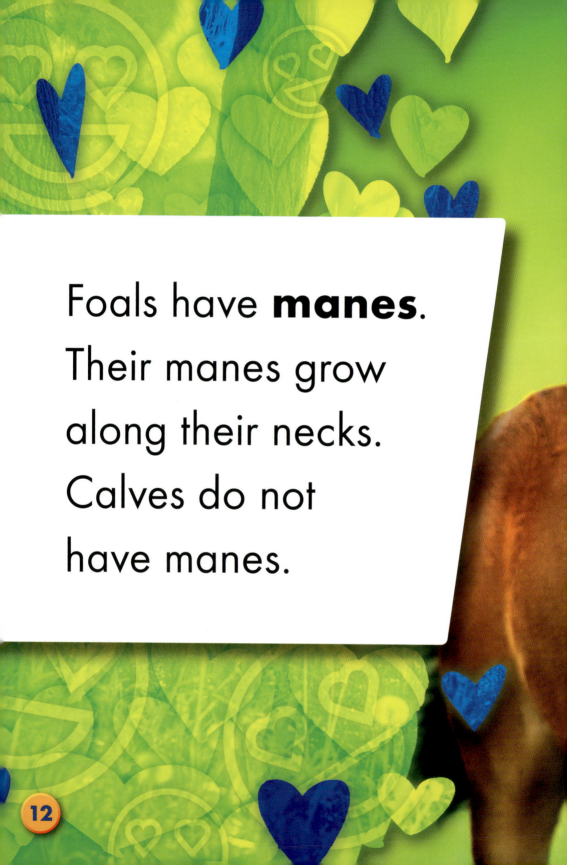

Foals have **manes**. Their manes grow along their necks. Calves do not have manes.

Both babies have **hooves**. Foal hooves have one toe. Calf hooves have two toes!

Stables and Barns

Some foals live in **stables**. Others live in barns. Most calves live in barns.

stable

barn

Foals neigh.
Calves moo.
Which farm baby
do you think is cuter?

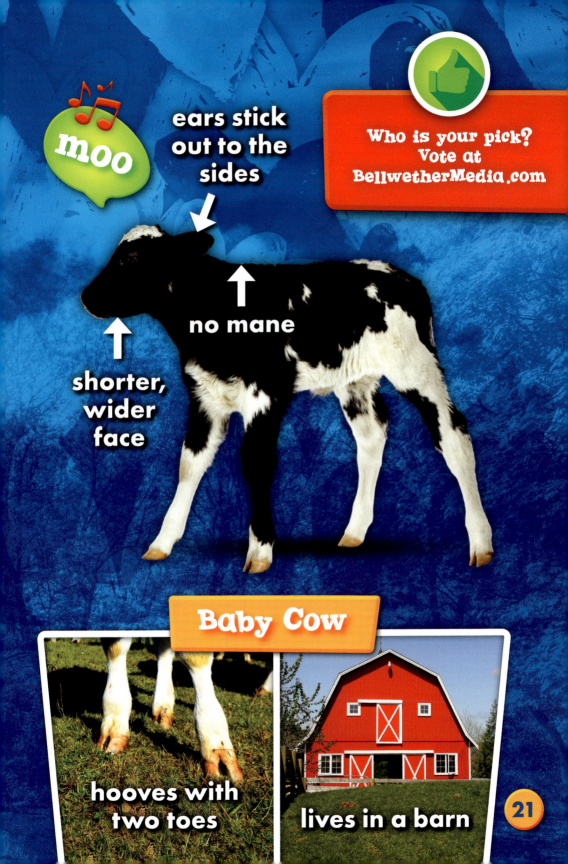

Glossary

compare

to see how things are alike or different

manes

long hair on the necks of horses

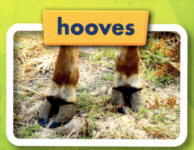

hooves

hard coverings on the feet of some animals

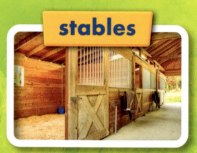

stables

buildings with stalls where horses live

To Learn More

AT THE LIBRARY

Barnes, Rachael. *Baby Cows*. Minneapolis, Minn.: Bellwether Media, 2023.

Hicks, Kelli. *Born On a Farm*. New York, N.Y.: Crabtree Publishing, 2023.

Rathburn, Betsy. *Baby Horses*. Minneapolis, Minn.: Bellwether Media, 2022.

ON THE WEB

FACTSURFER

Factsurfer.com gives you a safe, fun way to find more information.

1. Go to www.factsurfer.com.

2. Enter "baby horse or baby cow" into the search box and click.

3. Select your book cover to see a list of related content.

Index

barns, 16, 17
cows, 4, 5, 6
ears, 10
faces, 8
farms, 4, 18
hooves, 14, 15
horses, 4, 5, 6
manes, 12, 13
moo, 18, 19
necks, 12
neigh, 18, 19
stables, 16, 17
toes, 14, 15

The images in this book are reproduced through the courtesy of: Marlinda vs Spek/ Adobe Stock, front cover (foal); Jasmijn Fotografeert, front cover (calf); GlobalP, pp. 3 (foal), 21 (calf); Eric Isselee, pp. 3 (calf), 20 (foal); kyslynskahal, pp. 4-5, 19; emholk, p. 5; imv, pp. 6-7; Brinja Schmidt, p. 7; acceptfoto, pp. 8-9; Nataphat Kaewsanchai, p. 9; Qvist2000, pp. 10-11; Callipso88, p. 11; Nemyrivskyi Viacheslav, pp. 12-13; treasurephoto, p. 13; Wirestock, pp. 14-15; Plotitsyna NiNa, p. 15; pfluegler-photo, pp. 16-17; Deb Drury, p. 17; Volodymyr Burdiak, pp. 18-19; Nature Picture Library / Alamy Stock Photo/ Alamy, p. 20 (hooves with one toe); Chen's Photos, p. 20 (lives in a stable or barns); YAY Media AS / Alamy Stock Photo/ Alamy, p. 21 (hooves with two toes); Solidago, p. 21 (lives in a barn); CatMicroStock, p. 22 (compare); Pornsawan Baipakdee, p. 22 (hooves); mkant, p. 22 (manes); Artazum, p. 22 (stables).